Brightbeams of Jesus
Among the Burning Sands

Ilissa Ritchie

AB ASPECT Books
www.ASPECTBooks.com

Copyright © 2014 ASPECT Books
ISBN-13: 978-1-4796-0451-7 (Paperback)
ISBN-13: 978-1-4796-0452-4 (ePub)
ISBN-13: 978-1-4796-0453-1 (Mobi)
Library of Congress Control Number: 2014919775

Published by

AB **ASPECT Books**
www.ASPECTBooks.com

Table of Contents

All names marked with an asterisk (*) are pseudonyms.

Chapter One

One day when I was thirteen years old, my older brother Claude* came to me and asked, "Hey, Sis, want to work with me today?"

Wow! I thought. *MONEY!*

"Sure," I said.

Claude and I were picked up by his boss, Fred*. It was a short drive to the work site, and once we arrived we got busy taking care of the job at hand. Our job consisted of moving car batteries from one place to another. After working for a while, Fred called me over to where he was standing. When I was within arm's-length, he stuffed money into my bra and pants. I don't remember what he said while doing this, but anger rose within me, and I shouted, "Take me home right now!"

I ran away from him and went to find my brother. I finally located him in the employee break room. He was alone, so I cried and told him the whole story. Claude simply said, "Please don't tell Mom!"

Claude always said that when he didn't want to get in trouble. Earlier in the year Claude asked my little sister Helen* to sit between his legs. He then began to fondle her. As soon as Helen realized what he was doing, she broke free from his grasp and ran away. Claude yelled behind her, "Don't tell Mom!"

Another time he invited Helen and I to come inside his fort. He said, "We are going to play a game. Just take off your clothes and come inside." Then Claude closed the door.

I told Helen to run as fast as we could to get away from him. As we retreated, we could hear Claude yelling, "Don't tell Mom."

In spite of these traumatic experiences, I could hear Jesus calling me and saying, "Don't be afraid—I am here; I am with you."

Chapter Two

Our dad, Doug*, was born in 1916 in the eastern United States. His mother, Jean*, divorced her husband when dad was six months old, and by the time he was two, mother and son had settled in Beverly Hills, California. The years flew by, and dad enrolled at Beverly Hills High School where he learned how to read and write music. At the age of twelve, dad wrote his first song. After high school dad played for Bing Crosby at the Santa Anita horse race track. He also played with Frank Sinatra, Benny Goodman, and Louis Armstrong. Dad even played for Dwight D. Eisenhower at the Ocotilla Lodge in Palm Springs, California. General Eisenhower sat with Dad, and they sang together while surrounded by General Eisenhower's men. Another time when Dad was playing the piano at a restaurant, Howard Hughes and his girlfriend came in and rented the whole place for the entire night just to hear Dad play piano without a crowd! That night Dad was tipped $100.00 per hour!

In addition to playing the piano, Dad raised Pinto Saddlebred horses. Since he had been a little boy, he had ridden horses. After graduating from high school, Dad got some horses to train. Someone traded a Palomino for one of Dad's horses. Dad did not want the Palomino, but he took it, which turned out to be a good choice because a young man named Roy Rogers came by one day and needed a horse to work in the movies. Dad and Mr. Rogers worked out a deal, and Trigger became famous. Dad raised several other horses: Longstreet, a stallion that went to Africa, Vanity Fair, Society's Top Spot, Golden Revelation, Kilarney Blue Skies, Corsican Bandit, El Ray Manchado, April Chief, and Wild Chance. My own pony, Everything Nice, and Helen's pony, Pone Pone, won awards in local parades when we were growing up.

Mom was also born in the East. Her father, Ed^, was a descendent of royalty, but he died of tuberculosis, along with his baby son. My mom was six years old at the time her dad died. Her mother later died of a brain tumor. In her early twenties my mom, Faye*, married Mr. Lee*, and they both joined the Navy. Sadly, Mr. Lee died, and after six months my mom received an honorable discharge and left the Navy. She then got a job teaching roller skating. Although it was a fun job, it ended in disgrace when her boss raped her one day after class. She decided to keep the child, but she later left the baby boy with her ailing mother and joined the Mafia as one of the leader's girlfriends. She became pregnant again and gave birth to a violet-eyed, black haired boy. The Mafia leader did not want Mom to have any part in raising his child, so Mom signed paperwork giving up her rights to her son.

By this time my mom had met my dad, and they were dating. A few years later the Mafia contacted Mom and asked to see her. They said the child was not "right." Dad took Mom to the appointed meeting location. When she entered the house, a woman brought the young child out. When he saw Mom, he cried, "Mommy, Mommy!" Before Mom could hold her child, the woman grabbed the child and said, "Oh! He is alright after all." They told Mom to leave. Weeping, she left and climbed into the car with Dad.

The baggage Mom and Dad brought to their marriage and our family weighed heavily on us as children.

Chapter Three

When Mom and Dad married, they lived in a ranch house on Clancy Lane in Rancho Mirage, California. The home was surrounded with rose bushes and trees. At this time Jay was around two years old and was living with my parents instead of with his grandmother, whom Mom had left him with when she joined the Mafia.

Dad took good care of Jay and bought him a rocking horse, a tricycle, and the cutest car that he could "drive" all over the yard. Four years later my brother Claude was born. Claude was Dad's first boy child, so he doted on him even more than Jay. Dad's mother, Jean, acted the same way as he did, falling all over Claude and bringing him gifts while ignoring Jay. Little Jay stood by feeling rejected while Claude got a rocking horse, a red wagon, a tricycle, a pool, and other special gifts from his grandmother.

I was born just nine months after Claude, so when Grandma came with all the gifts for Claude, I was just little. One time when Claude was being doted on by Grandma, Jay hit Claude, and then Claude hit me, and I kicked the cat! Mom saw the whole affair, and told Jean to leave and never return. We never saw our only living grandmother again.

Thanks to my mom's service in the Navy, even though it was short, she and Dad were able to buy five acres of pure white rolling sand dunes. Around this time my little sister Helen was born. They built a ranch house with a rock fireplace and a glass hallway that had vines of beautiful flowers growing near it. There was a wooden porch with purple and white flowers, against the big picture window.

Jay, Claude, Helen, and I loved the sand dunes. We had only one old neighbor about a block away. Other people just built desert shacks to claim their properties. There were no trees near us, only creosote bushes, which we called greasewood bushes because the tiny leaves were always greasy. Dad planted giant athel tamarisk trees as a wind block for our house. The trees lined the left side of the property. Then Dad planted oleander bushes out front, which always bloomed white, pink, and purple. Dad also lined our driveway with pepper trees. We even had a Japanese oleander that bloomed yellow. On the side of the house a bougainvillea vine grew beautiful and brilliant. The vine had the most radiant magenta flowers. We also had a palo verde bush that Dad had trained to be a tree. The leaves felt like rice paper. In back of the house, Dad planted eucalyptus trees. Dad even planted a jujube tree in the front yard. At the end of the driveway there was a blue gray smoke tree. It was so small the horned toads liked to burrow underneath the bush.

Early in the morning, Claude and I would begin our chores, which included feeding the horses and chickens. Dad usually worked all night playing the piano, and Mom was drinking a lot by now in an effort to drown out the past. After we finished our chores, Helen would wake up, and we would head outside. She or I do not remember eating breakfast or lunch—all we remember is that we had to stay outside until supper.

With acres of sand dunes surrounding us, we had lots of fun outside. With Mom drunk, no one combed our hair or helped us get dressed. Most of the time we ran around in just our under clothes! In the morning the sand was cool, and we could chase each other, sinking up to our knees in the sand, and play without getting too hot. In addition to playing, we would explore the footprints and tracks in the sand for lizards, bugs, snakes, birds, Jack rabbits, coyotes, scorpions, and horned toads.

Helen and I also found other ways to have fun. We took a long straight board and put it through the horses fence to make a teeter-totter for ourselves. But as the day wore on the sand absorbed the sunlight, and it got blazing hot. We then spent time running from the shade of one greasewood bush to another. As we ran our feet burned with every step. Sometimes we didn't think we could make it to the next bush, but we did not cry. To our surprise, the rattlesnakes and sidewinder snakes had the same idea. They would hide under the greasewood bushes because the sand was too hot. I remember finding a stick so I could poke at the snakes to hear the rattle and hiss. I thought it was fun, never imagining how much danger we were in!

When the sun would start to go down, the sand would cool off again. Then the three of us would start to dig in the sand. The more you dug, the more sand would fill in the hole, so we would start digging faster and faster. Then Mom would call for us to come in to take a bath and eat, but often we would stay outside until a scorpion was dug up. We all got stung at different times!

Finally, we would go in and take a bath. Then we would eat supper, watch TV, and go to bed. Once we were in bed, Mom and Dad often got in yelling matches.

Chapter Four

One day our Dad found a foxhound named Suzy. Suzy had been trained to hunt mountain lions. She would track them, but when she saw the big cat, she would turn and run. So Suzy came to our house. I loved the way she ran on the sand dunes trying to catch the huge jack rabbits. We had trouble with the coyotes getting into the chicken pen, but when Suzy came, she found great delight in tracking down the coyotes and killing them. In the morning we would look outside and see dead coyotes by the front door. We often tied Suzy up so she wouldn't run around howling on the sand dunes.

In addition to Suzy, we had two cats: Rowe Rowe and Tiger. Rowe Rowe was a long-haired black and white cat, but a black widow spider bit him and he died. Tiger was a short-haired black cat, but Dad caught Tiger scratching his trees, so Dad put Tiger in a sack, tied the top, and dropped him somewhere in the middle of the desert. I cried, but Dad insisted that the cat would be fine.

Sometimes during the spring it would rain for two days! When the rain stopped, we had so much fun on the sand dunes. We could build roads and big cities. Claude had some cars, and we would drive the cars everywhere. But the best fun was sliding down the dunes on an old water ski. The three of us would take turns climbing to the top of a dune, sitting on the ski, and being pushed down the slope! We did this again and again without seeming to get tired. Soon after the rain all the dormant flower seeds would begin to bloom. The white dunes were now carpeted in purple verbena, and a small white desert lily. The sand dunes were a beautiful canopy of color!

During the winter it would drop to fifty degrees, and we froze! But our rock fireplace always kept us warm. Going out to hunt for firewood among the greasewood was not an easy job. I remember going from bush to bush hoping to find a dead branch somewhere, and it was cold.

Things at home slowly grew worse the older we got. Claude tried to fondle us girls, and no one was aware of what was going on. Jay was always sweet to Helen and me, but Mom made him leave home when he turned eighteen. Mom and Dad yelled more and more. I often slipped out of the house at night and stood in my night-gown and let the wind blow threw my long brown hair as a means of escaping the chaos inside the house. The wind would be so loud that I wouldn't be able to hear anything else.

Chapter Five

When Claude was thirteen, I was twelve, and Helen was eight, Dad and Mom got a divorce. Mom received custody of us kids, but we had to find a place to live. We moved from place to place before finally settling in a one-bedroom apartment in Palm Desert, California. This is where Claude had me work with him and his boss. I didn't tell Mom what happened, but I'm not sure it would have done much good if I had. Mom would drink all night, yell at us, and then sleep all day. Because of her habits, I was responsible for making our school lunches, getting Claude and Helen up, and making sure we all got off to school. When we came home, I was responsible for making dinner while Mom, Claude, and Helen watched TV. I often got angry. I did not think it was fair, but I still cooked dinner.

At this time on the weekends Claude taught me how to break into houses. He also taught me how to steal from stores. I knew it was wrong, but I still stole candy from stores. Along with this bad habit, I was also swearing worse than a sailor. I felt depressed and alone, and I wanted to die. At age fifteen I was in high school at Indio High, while Claude had dropped out and was working. I discovered that I loved art. I liked painting or working with clay. I was fascinated by mermaids, and one day I made one out of clay, burned in green and gold. I didn't know that it was the idol of the Philistines in the Bible known as Dagon, a merman or fish god. Another extracurricular activity that Helen and I were in together was choir.

My high school counselor was a Seventh-day Adventist, and so was one of our teachers. By my junior year I was introduced to a family that had a mom and dad and two little kids. They were dressed nice and did not smoke or drink or yell! They often fed us, and I remember them playing nicc music at their home. They also introduced us to a study called "The Man From Way Out." As I took the studies, I learned that I did not come from a monkey! The story of Creation didn't have any holes in it like evolution did!

My mom got jealous of this couple, and in a rage she told me to move in with them, which was fine with me. As I went to walk out the door, she called me back. When my dad found out, he came to our apartment and proceeded to call me a slut and a whore. He forbid me from going to the couple's house and said that I was no longer a part of his family because of the new things I was learning. Praise God, He alone kept me calm. After he yelled at me, Dad left and went to the couple's home and yelled at them!

Because of my interaction with the couple, I learned to thank God for my food. At home I would even offer the blessing; however, Mom always laughed at me. One day as I prepared to eat something at home, I bowed my head to have the blessing. As I prayed I felt the most wonderful, loving, kind, bright, gentle hand touch my shoulder. A feeling of peace and the deepest love washed over me. I looked up and ran to the door, but no one was there. After that experience, without a shadow of a doubt, I knew Jesus was real and was watching over me.

Around that time I was invited to go to the Indio Seventh-day Adventist Church. They started an evangelistic series with Pastor Carney and the Heritage Singers, and I was able to attend every meeting. Everything made perfect sense. The love of God soothed my troubled soul. The songs gave me such peace. I knew that nothing could be more beautiful than the love of God. When they had an alter call, I went forward. After some additional study, I was baptized by

Pastor R. L. Watts and joined the Seventh-day Adventist church. Praise God!

Because of the great, persistent, enduring love of Jesus, all my swearing, stealing, arguing, and lying vanished. I wanted to live forever loving Jesus and obeying His commandments. To emphasize how far our sins were removed, the couple who showed me the first glimpse of Jesus had us right down all our sins on a piece of paper. I thought about all my sins, and selfishness was the root to every one of them. That is what I put on the paper. Then the couple lit a fire, and I tossed my paper in the fire. That exercise taught me that I was completely forgiven by my precious friend Jesus. The first Bible verse I memorized was 1 John 1:9: "If we confess our sins, he is faithful and just to forgive us our sins, and to cleanse us from all unrighteousness."

Chapter Six

I was still a junior in high school, but my whole outlook on life had changed now that I knew Jesus. I enjoyed having prayer between classes and Bible studies off campus. I argued with my teachers about evolution, and told the teacher, Creation made more sense. In my psychology class the teacher brought out a Ouija board for us to use. I was not the only Christian in the class, and we quickly joined together to pray that the evil spirits would leave our classroom.

The school also started a "Bible class," which I enrolled in. On the first day the teacher asked us to come up with a skit from the book of Job. He said, "God can be the Mafia leader!"

I stood up and said, "This is not a Bible class!"

The teacher responded, "The Bible is just a book of literature."

I immediately felt that the class was a blaspheme to our God, so I told the teacher I was dropping his class. I was just a young Christian, but I was on fire for God and standing up for Him.

The Indio SDA Church decided to send me to a spiritual retreat at Pine Springs Ranch in the mountains. It was so beautiful! I loved seeing the tall pine trees and huge lodge. Everyone was so kind and happy! We studied the Bible and sang songs. The testimonies were beautiful and inspiring. Before I knew it the weekend was over, and everyone began packing up and leaving. A family from the church had taken me to the ranch, so I had to wait for them to return. Within a few hours everyone was gone, and the cleaning crew had shown up. I felt abandoned and alone and somewhat frightened. Suddenly I saw a butterfly flying around. As it flew toward me, I held out my hand, and it landed right on my palm! The beautiful creature stayed with me until my ride came. Once again God was assuring me of His sweet, sweet presence.

At times my mom gave me glimpses of who she could be. She told Helen and I she once saved two baby sparrows. She said she raised them, and when they were grown, she taught them to fly. She loved all God's creatures, and they loved her. This was definitely a gentler side than I had seen growing up when she was drunk.

During my junior year Mom took a class from Henri Mancini, an American conductor and composer, at the College of the Desert. Mom played the cello, and he told her he loved the way she played with real passion. He gave her an autographed picture of himself, and they became good friends. One time an orchestra was playing at the College of the Desert, and Mom and I went to listen. We heard pieces by Wagner, Strauss, Bach, and even Beethoven! I loved every moment of that evening with Mom.

One day my counselor called me into his office. After I sat down, he told me I had enough credits to graduate high school that year as a junior! I just needed to complete one class that summer at the College of the Desert. It made sense to go to college rather than take one class my senior year, so I said yes! As graduation approached, Mom went out and bought me a new dress, which was actually a pink housecoat. She was drunk when she went shopping, so I'm not sure she realized what she had purchased.

By now Claude had dropped out of school and Helen was working, so when graduation night I didn't expect them to attend. However, I hoped Mom would come watch me receive my diploma. I asked her if she was coming, but she said she was too tired. My boyfriend at the time and his mom took me—they even bought me a present, a picture of Christ walking with two disciples after

He rose from the dead. Graduation was a special experience, but when we took off our robes, some of the other kids laughed at my housecoat. Their teasing hurt, but I should have been used to it by now. I was thankful that Jesus was there with me. I knew He loved me no matter what I wore. I held onto His promise that He was always with me: "Lo, I am with you always, even unto the end of the world" (Matt. 28:20).

During the summer, I took a class in art history at the College of the Desert and devoted my spare time to singing with a group of friends—Harry, Gary, and Sue, and a few others. We called ourselves The New Advent Singers, and we often spent our weekend traveling to different churches on Sabbath to sing for the worship service or an afternoon program. I loved praising the Lord through music and being with fellow believers. It was a balm to my soul as I looked out over the audience and saw everyone's smiling faces as we sang about God's love for us. I pray I will see all those precious souls in heaven.

Chapter Seven

The next year I enrolled at Loma Linda University's La Sierra campus with a goal of becoming an evangelistic artist. To help pay for school, I worked on the grounds crew taking care of the plants and keeping the campus looking beautiful. I also took out some loans and grants that allowed me to stay in school. One of my favorite classes was "The Life of Christ," which was taught by Pastor Morris Venden and Madaline Haldeman, a Greek teacher at the school. They were both filled with God's Holy Spirit, and I was so blessed. I absorbed everything they said, and I fell deeper in love with God. I could have taken their class over again and again.

College was such a new experience for me. My life was completely different compared to a few years before. I could hold Bible studies at the dorm, and no one would get angry! I could wake before dawn, dress, exercise, have morning Bible study with a few girls, get ready for my day, and eat breakfast. After growing up with only dinner, I enjoyed eating breakfast! God is so good! Then I headed off to classes. Interspersed in my day were lunch and dinner. I was spoiled eating three meals a day, and I praised God for His provision.

During my first year of college, I met a twelve-year-old girl named Kay*. Just one look at her eyes and the manner in which she dressed, and God impressed me of a horrid, terrifying past. In the heat of summer, she never took off her jean jacket. I wanted to hold her and love her and tell her that I understood, but she was so fragile. Over time we became friends, and I determined to show her the love of God and His saving power to change your life and help you move beyond your circumstances. Around that time I also determined, no matter how long it took, even decades, that I would pray for the salvation of my family and friends.

Before long young men began to ask me out. I certainly had not come from a home that modeled a good marriage—a marriage built on God. I determined to marry only if the young man was a Seventh-day Adventist and had come from a home with parents who were also Adventists. I also determined that this young man's parents must still be happily married. Finally, I wanted the approval of my heavenly Father.

Many of the young men did not meet my hidden request, so I politely dismissed their invitations. Soon a tall, red-headed young man approached me, and we became friends. I met his parents who were Adventists and still happily married. He met the requirements, but he always walked five feet away from me, and he would sit about three persons away from me.

Then one night he opened up to me and shared with me his whole life story. By the end of the conversation he told me that I was the only girl for him. That night after I returned to the quiet of my room, I fell on my knees and talked to my friend Jesus. I asked Him if there was anyone else or if he was the right one. That night God gave me a dream in which I was talking to my husband, but it wasn't the nice boy that I had just spent the evening with. The man in my dream was tall with brown hair and brown eyes. The next day the red-headed young man and I were walking to a nearby neighborhood to host a Branch Sabbath School with some other students. Before we reached our destination, another young man stopped us and said the leader was running late and we would have to start the program without her. The red-headed young man played banjo and the driver of the car had a guitar. As I got in the car and looked at the driver, I recognized him as the man in my dream!

I silently praised God for answering my prayer and showing me who I should marry. I immediately asked the young man his name, where he worked, and where he lived. I also learned that that day was Dean's* birthday. I could barely contain my excitement. When we arrived at the location for the meeting we got out of the car, and I turned my attention to those in attendance. The two young men played their instruments and led out in the singing, after which I told a Bible story about the golden calf from Exodus 32.

Chapter Eight

Although God had given me a dream that Dean was to be my husband, we did not immediately start dating, or even hanging out together. The school year finished, and summer arrived. I obtained a job working with Community Crusade Against Drugs (CCAD). As part of our job responsibilities, we divided up the city of Riverside, California, which is next to La Sierra, and passed out literature warning about the dangers of drugs. My leader was Will James. He would take one side of the street, and I would work the other. I pray that many of the precious souls which I met that summer will be in heaven.

Will's wife was pregnant, and I planned a baby shower for her. As the guests arrived on the day of the baby shower, I was surprised to see Dean enter the room. But he had someone with him, who I soon discovered was his old girlfriend. I asked if he could stay and take pictures, and he agreed. A few days later, we spent Friday and Sabbath together, and I met his wonderful parents. They were so cute as they peeked around the door to "spy" on Dean and I as we watched old home movies.

As we talked I learned that his old girlfriend's brother had pleaded with Dean to go back with his sister. That night I fell on my knees and cried. Through my tears I asked God to bless Dean and his old girlfriend if that was God's plan. I asked Him to help me accept His will, not mine.

With a few weeks left in the summer, I decided to visit my mom and Helen in the desert. While staying with them I received a letter from Dean telling me that he had broken up with his old girlfriend and wanted to know if I would be interested in getting to know him better. Wow, was I ever! My return letter knocked his socks off. Mom and Helen decided to move to La Sierra to be closer to me. Back in the area, Dean and I began to spend lots of time together. Every day was heaven with him. I even introduced Kay to Dean. Life seemed perfect!

One night Dean told me he loved me. I was in the clouds! Of course, I told him I loved him too. The next day Dean announced that we were officially boyfriend and girlfriend. After a while my Mom thought seeing each other every day was too much, so she told me I had to stay away from Dean for one whole week—that was one of the longest weeks of my life. On Halloween the college had a pray meeting, and Mom asked me to find a ride home. Our week was not up, but Dean took me home and asked me to marry him. I told him that I would say yes on three conditions: if my mom said yes, if my dad said yes, and if God said yes. Praise God my mom said yes. I phoned my dad, and sight unseen he said yes. Of course, I already knew God's answer, so after receiving conformation from my parents, I told Dean that it would give me great pleasure to be his wife. We got married later that year on March 23, 1975.

After we were married, I had to drop out of college because of how much I owed. I got a full-time job at the College Market in La Sierra. While working there I learned of the horrible plight of the Christians in Russia through a magazine I received called *Underground Evangelism*. I was touched by their stories, so I asked Dean if there was any way we could help them. Together we agreed to send half of my paycheck to Russia. With my interest piqued for Russia, I purchased a book called *The Persecutor* by Sergei Kordikov. He had persecuted Russian Christians until God called him to the faith, much like Saul who became Paul. Much later God allowed me to meet the publisher of *Underground Evangelism*. Praise our precious Savior for His watch care over all

His children and for placing it upon our hearts to support one another in the faith, even when we are separated by oceans.

Kay's situation was getting really serious, and I prayed about what role God wanted me to play in her life. Around this time, Dean and I moved to a one-bedroom apartment for a short time; then we moved to another apartment with two bedrooms. After we got settled in the two-bedroom apartment, Kay moved in with us. Her dad helped pay for us to keep her as a foster daughter. Her pain and humiliation started when she was a baby and did not stop until she joined us at thirteen years of age.

Our first Christmas with Kay was nothing short of delightful. We let her pick out a live Christmas tree, and Dean cut it down. When we got back to the apartment with the tree, we had to cut off the bottom and some of the top just to get it in the apartment! Helen and Dean's parents came over to celebrate. Dean took a photo of Helen sitting next to the Christmas tree. Then, pointing the camera a little to the right, he took my picture next to the Christmas tree. When we developed the pictures, you had to put Helen and my picture together to see the width of the tree! We couldn't put on angel on top because the top of the tree touched the ceiling! That Christmas we laughed and enjoyed each other's company and love. We showered Kay with gifts and things she never had before such as a nightgown, a robe, a coat, and other things. The joy and beauty of that Christmas will remain in my heart forever.

Chapter Nine

Later we moved to another home with a finished attic. While Kay was away at boarding school, Helen moved in and stayed for a while before eventually moving back to Palm Desert where she got a job busing tables at a restaurant she began working at when she was fifteen. She was eighteen now, and while working one day a guy from New York offered for her to come stay with him and see some Broadway shows. She took him up on the offer and he booked a plane ticket to New York City. When she arrived she discovered his real intentions were to use her as a call girl. She turned around and got out of there, although she changed her return ticket and flew to Kentucky to see our dad.

During this time Dean and I were praying earnestly for Helen, pleading with God to save her.

After visiting Dad she returned to La Sierra to be with us. We were going to the Riverside Seventh-day Adventist Church at the time. Pastor Tomlin was our senior pastor, and Pastor Jim was our youth pastor. We praised God when Helen gave her heart to Jesus and was baptized by Pastor Tomlin. After her conversion she got a job working at Loma Linda University's La Sierra campus doing what I had done—Community Crusade Against Drugs.

Through united prayers we watched Mom also come to Jesus. She stopped drinking, smoking, and yelling! The transformation was remarkable. We praised God once again for saving another member of my family and fulfilling the promise of John 10:28, 29: "And I give unto them eternal life; and they shall never perish, neither shall any man pluck them out of my hand. My Father, which gave them me, is greater than all; and no man is able to pluck them out of my Father's hand." What determined, persistent, love the Father has for His children—deeper and stronger than we can imagine.

When Kay finished up her year at boarding academy, she moved back in with us. Dean often took her for a ride on his dad's motorcycle, which she loved. She began calling us her new mom and dad! With Kay back at home, the three of us enjoyed camping trips to Dark Canyon in the mountains of Idyllwild, climbing up the waterfalls, and washing our hair with biodegradable shampoo. We also had fun going to Disneyland and Knott's Berry Farm amusement parks. We traveled to the beach and enjoyed many other summer activities. But the most precious times we spent together were when we sang for the elderly at rest homes in our area.

We loved singing along with the Heritage Singers. When Helen came back, the four of us would sing Heritage Singer songs at church. (Helen even tried out to sing with them!) We tried to go to every concert in our area, and we tried to collect all of their records. We were privileged to be in the audience when the Heritage Singers recorded their ten-year reunion record at the Swing Auditorium.

One day in the fall Dean and I had just come back from camping at Pine Springs Ranch. It was cold, so Dean started a fire in our fireplace. We had an old wood shake roof that was in bad repair. Suddenly a car drove up to our house, and they blasted their horn. When we looked out the window, we could see flames reflecting on their windshield. We called the fire department, and they came right away. The whole top of the house was on fire. All of Kay's things burned in the fire. Although the fire did not spread downstairs, we sustained a lot of water damage. In spite of the loss, we praised God that Kay had not been home and no one had been hurt in the fire.

Kay went back to her original home, and we went to Dean's parents' home. One day not too long after the fire I put too much laundry in his mom's machine, and for the first time she yelled at me. I ran out the door and ended up at the burned home. Dean found me there, crying. I felt so homeless and afraid. He took me home to his parents' home, and that night God gave me a dream and showed me our new home. Within three months God brought us to the house in my dream, and we moved in. We were so thankful to be back in our own place with Kay again.

We had to fix and repair the bathroom and the master bedroom, but we were soon settled in and it felt like home. Dean and I had been married five years and were longing for children of our own. One night I received another dream in which I saw Dean carrying a little boy on his shoulders. It wasn't long after that that I became pregnant. I once again marveled at the fact that my heavenly Father loved me enough to communicate with me.

At the same time we started a Bible study group with a neighbor and some friends. We were all Seventh-day Adventists who longed to be closer to Jesus. Our neighbor got pregnant before I did. She had a midwife who worked under a doctor in case there was an emergency. When she was ready to deliver, her child came out with the cord wrapped around its neck. The midwife saved the baby and our friend. Because of this experience, Dean and I chose to use the same midwife. We met the doctor and then checked in with the midwife throughout the pregnancy. My water broke Christmas night, and after six hours of labor, our midwife and her coach came to our house. They helped me to breath right, and before I knew it I was holding our baby girl! We named her Rachel*. At this time Helen was married and pregnant with her first child, which turned out to be a baby boy. Helen and her husband lived in Lancaster, California.

Chapter Ten

Kay immediately bonded with Rachel. She loved to babysit and take baby Rachel to the park. I also enjoyed taking Rachel to the park to play. It felt so good giving and receiving love.

While I was pregnant with Rachel, Dean injured his back at work. He was moving a pole with a yard of concrete at the bottom, and when he went to put the pole in the hole, he fell in with it. His sweaty hands did not let go of the pipe. He was in so much pain, but the doctors found no broken bones. However, one test showed that all of his pain was in his lower back. Our precious Kay spent more than $400 dollars buying Dean a piece of medical equipment that enabled him to hang upside down and stretch his back, which was a tremendous help in relieving his back pain.

We experienced another medical emergency when Rachel was eight months old that turned out to be a blessing in disguise. Rachel broke her leg, but when the doctor was casting her leg he noticed a two-toned mole under my arm. He looked at it more closely and said it needed to be removed immediately. The next day I had a procedure done to remove the mole, and the doctor discovered that it was melanoma cancer. The doctor said if they had not seen the mole I would have died in six months. I praised God for His providence and watch care.

When Rachel was two years old I became pregnant again. I had the same midwife, but this time when my water broke our little boy got stuck—he was two pounds heavier than Rachel. Fortunately, in the end Jesse* came out just fine.

One year later we sold our house in California and moved to Kentucky. The area in which we lived was becoming too dangerous, and my Dad was not saved yet, so we felt that it was time to move. Kay was twenty-one now and had her own apartment, so off we went to Kentucky. When we got to Kentucky, I watched Dean put Jesse on his shoulders and walk through the fields. The dream God sent me before we had children had finally come true. The children loved the ducks, geese, horses, cows, cats, and dogs on my dad's fifty-acre farm.

Chapter Eleven

When the children were small, I decided to become a literature evangelist (LE). I went door-to-door selling Uncle Arthur's Bedtime stories, *The Great Controversy*, and *The Desire of Ages*. I also left sample books in doctors' offices and other places. There were cards inside to send in, and I followed up on any of the interest cards that I received in the mail. With every home that I visited and each person that I talked to, I longed for them to know my friend Jesus. I always carried a sample book of stories with me that people could buy for $5.00. I sold many of those stories.

One time I drove to Lebanon, Kentucky, in search of a prospective customer. I drove through the whole town, but didn't find the address of where I needed to be. After going through the little town, I came to a crossroad with nothing in front of me and nothing to the left or right. I went to turn around, and I heard a Voice say, "Turn left."

"There is nothing out here!" I said out loud, so I went to turn around.

Then I heard the Voice say, "Turn left."

"OK, OK," I said.

I turned left, but I still saw nothing. Then a little farther up the road I saw a trailer park on my right and a Kroger on my left. I drove into the Kroger parking lot to use the pay phone. I discovered that the customer I was looking for was across the street in the trailer park. She wanted the Bedtime Stories, but she didn't have any money, so I gave her a sample book.

God led me to that woman because she needed a book about Him. That wasn't the only instance where God protected and guided me. Another time a car from the opposite direction tried to pass me on a skinny road. I tried to pull over, but my car slid on the loose gravel, sending my vehicle toward the twenty-foot drop to the dry river bed below! The next thing I knew my car's front end was sitting on the dry river bed. I climbed out of the car unhurt! The headlights were not even smashed! The front end was not even dented! I may not have seen angels, but I know that they guided my car and let me down easy. I climbed back up to the road and called a tow truck driver who managed to retrieve my car from the ravine. I praised God for His protection once again.

While working as an LE I had the chance to go to a spiritual retreat at Indian Creek Camp with other LEs. The drive from Kentucky to Tennessee was beautiful. I was alone, but Dean had just checked out the car. When I was almost to the camp, my brakes started to go out. I quickly stopped the car because it was downhill to the camp entrance. One of the other LEs stopped and said to use him as a bumper. I started the car but went real slow, using the other car and my hand brake as a means to keep me going a safe speed. I made it down to the camp and the other LEs put in a new master cylinder for the brakes. That weekend I marked Psalm 63:6, 7 in my Bible—"When I remember thee upon my bed, and meditate on thee in the night watches. Because thou hast been my help, therefore in the shadow of thy wings will I rejoice."

I worked as an LE for one year, and then decided to stay home full time with Rachel and Jesse.

We spent six years with my Dad and his new wife, Sue*. I learned to milk a cow, start a fire in the wood stove, and have fun with the children.

One day I heard that my mom had passed away. Dean and I and the kids drove out to California. Helen flew in with a friend. We were the only ones who came to the funeral service. We received flowers from the church, and Helen and I bought flowers. It was a small ceremony, I put roses in my mom's hands, one for every child she had. Since she had been in the Navy, she was buried at the national cemetery in Riverside, California. I was glad she was no longer suffering, and I knew that the next voice she will hear will be Jesus: "For the Lord himself shall descend from heaven with a shout, with the voice of the archangel, and with the trump of God: and the dead in Christ shall rise first: Then we which are alive and remain shall be caught up together with them in the clouds, to meet the Lord in the air: and so shall we ever be with the Lord" (1 Thess. 4:16, 17).

I can't wait for that day when Mom will be made brand new and will not experience any pain, sorrow, or bad memories. Instead, she will enjoy His love forever!

Chapter Twelve

After living with Dad for six years, we searched for a piece of land of our own and found fifteen acres in Meade County. The property was beautiful, especially in the spring when it was covered with yellow daffodils and white crocuses. When we left my dad's place, he became very angry and disowned me again. It hurt, but I prayed for him because I sincerely wanted my dad in heaven.

We purchased a double-wide modular home, and settled in on our new property. Unfortunately, after only a short time, the floors started to come up, the doors did not shut, and the walls bowed. We discovered that the plastic lining underneath the house was full of water. The company refused to fix it. Instead, they came and took the house away, and we were left homeless on our daughter's sixteenth birthday.

A friend in Louisville let Dean and I and Jesse live in their basement. Our pastor, Jim McConnell, had a friend in Tennessee who loaned us money to purchase another trailer. We praised God for once again working things out for our family.

On August 1, 1999, Dean and I and the kids drove across the country to California to see Dean's parents and friends. We were driving an old blue van, which proved faithful for long trips. We were thankful that Rachel could help us drive, for three drivers are better than two when you are driving 2,000 miles. We were in Joseph, New Mexico, and had stopped to get something to drink and snack on while we drove. I popped some gum in my mouth and slid in behind the steering wheel. I felt great even though I had not slept in quite some time.

Shortly after getting on the interstate, Rachel noticed that my head began to nod. Before she could say anything, the van began to weave in and out of the lane, and then it veered off the road and headed straight for a concrete pillar of a bridge. Rachel screamed my name, and I awoke and yelled Dean's name. Instinctively, he grabbed the steering wheel and turned it. We missed the concrete pillar by just a few inches and skidded on two wheels. Somehow we ended up parked on the side of the interstate. Two police officers arrived at the scene and asked how we had parked so perfectly on the interstate without rolling the vehicle after skidding. We told them our heavenly Father had spared our lives. The only thing that happened to the van was that the two tires we had skidded on were deflated and off the rim of the tire. Dean was able to get one of the tires back on the rim and inflated, and the other one we took off and used the spare.

After our trip out West, I returned to my job at Chick-fil-A. I enjoyed my work and coworkers. As always, I desired to share Jesus with others and tell them what He had done in my life. Some Catholic friends of mine were amazed that I could read my Bible. I longed for them to read on their own, but they said only the church could tell them the truth. I had another coworker ask me, "Does God really love me?" I told her God loved her so much. The company was closed every Sunday, but they let me have every Sabbath off.

Life was good, but there were also some health challenges that I had to deal with. When I was seventeen, I was diagnosed with asthma, which increasingly grew worse over the years and caused me to be hospitalized several times. At one point, I was using a breathing machine every hour or so. But God kept me breathing! I also had skin cancer two more times. Fortunately, both patches were removed before spreading.

Praise God that when He comes we will be made new! Paul wrote in 1 Corinthians 15:51 and 52 that "we shall all be changed, In a moment, in the twinkling of an eye, at the last trump: for the trumpet shall sound, and the dead shall be raised incorruptible, and we shall be changed."

Chapter Thirteen

In 2001 our lives changed forever. Dean's aging parents, Forrest* and Blanche*, required care and attention. Blanche had Alzheimer's disease, and Forrest had had a stroke and was struggling with reoccurring urinary tract infections. They were living in California and did not want to go to a nursing home, but Forrest also did not want to move. Dean and I prayed about the situation, got a leave of absence from where we were working, and hopped on a plane to California. We showed his parents beautiful pictures of Kentucky and pleaded with them to come live with us, but Forrest did not want to leave his home. Finally, I asked, "If your house sells, would you be willing to move?" Forrest said yes. The next day I spoke to the neighbor next door, and she came right over. I showed her the house, and it sold that day to her and her agent. Dean and I packed up the house with the help of Dean's sister, Rose, and we all headed for Kentucky.

When Dean and I reached Kentucky, we put their things in a storage unit. Forrest and Blanche arrived later by plane, and we got them settled into a nice apartment that they could pay for on a week-by-week basis until we could clear the land for a double-wide modular home on our property.

The University of Louisville had a program to help caregivers understand Alzheimer's disease that met at our church every three months. I was so grateful for the program and the support that the other members provided, for I was now Dean's parents full-time caregiver. I had some nurse's aid training in high school, but I appreciated the information I learned from the Alzheimer's meetings.

As their caregiver I cooked for them three times a day, gave them their pills, and took them to their doctor's appointments. Before long I realized I needed help. I knew one of my coworkers had worked with an Alzheimer's relative in Hawaii where she grew up, so I called Lily*.

After talking things over, Lily moved in with Forrest and Blanche in their three-bedroom modular home. One morning while I was caring for Forrest and Blanche, God impressed me to take a walk and spend some time talking with Him. I heeded the prompting and went outside.

After a while, Lily came out the door and stood on the porch with her mouth wide open. I asked her what was wrong, and she said she saw Jesus walking beside me. I hadn't seen anything, but I knew Jesus and His angels were with me every day. I praised God that He had manifested Himself in such a way for Lily. God wants to talk with us; He wants us to read the Bible every day so that we can draw closer to Him until we no longer see ourselves but we see Him.

With Forrest and Blanche settled into their new home, family and friends began to visit. Nephews, friends from California, and of course Rose all made plans to spend time with them. Dean's parents also enjoyed visits from our church members. We had a group of Spanish-speaking refugees from Cuba, Mexico, and San Salvador who held services in our fellowship hall. They enjoyed planning outings on our fifteen acres to hike, gather ferns, catch minnows, and spend time in nature! When they came to the property, the whole Spanish church would gather around Forrest's bed and pray for him.

Even though Lily was there to help out, I was still heavily involved in Forrest and Blanche's care. Forrest continued to struggle with repeated urinary tract infections. We took him to the doctor, and when the doctor took pictures of his bladder, it looked like a cave system. Our pastor and the elders of the church anointed Forrest.

Around this time Forrest had a pacemaker put in, and all too soon his kidneys started to fail and he was put on dialysis. I had to put Blanche in adult day care in order to take Forrest to dialysis. Lily continued to help with their care, but she struggled with panic attacks, especially in the car because she felt it was crowded. I also discovered that Lily was bipolar and was a diabetic. It was a challenge when I felt like I needed to take care of Lily and Dean's parents. She did help, especially in talking to Blanche when I couldn't take it anymore, listening to her speak like a broken record.

One day the dialysis doctors told me that Forrest was not getting better and the dialysis was not working any longer. Because he was almost completely deaf, I signed to him and asked him if he wanted to continue dialysis or just go home. I told him that if he went home, the doctors said he would die within five days. He chose to go home. I called the family, contacted the funeral home, and spoke with hospice. Poor Blanche did not understand what was happening. Rose flew out to say goodbye, but she could not stay because her son's wedding was that weekend. Rachel and Jesse also came home to say goodbye to their grandfather. On September 2 Forrest got restless and wanted to get out of his hospital bed and sit in a chair or on the couch. Once he was settled he fell asleep in Jesus. Forrest's nephew, a Seventh-day Adventist minister, held the funeral service.

Chapter Fourteen

After Forrest died, Lily stayed in her room and Blanche began to yell. When Lily did come out of her room, she would remind Blanche of her husband's death, which caused Blanche to relive the situation over again and again. I was emotional and physically exhausted and felt that I wanted to escape all of the drama of my life. One day I took Blanche to the day care without Lily. I then got in the car and planned to drive until I ran out of gas. I did not take my medication for my asthma, so I figured I would just stop breathing at some point and time while I drove.

As I drove I heard Jesus say to me, "Get something to eat." I decided to heed His voice, and I stopped and bought some food. I then drove to a park to eat, listen to gospel music, and read my Bible. Then an amazing thing happened:

several birds landed all around the van, a great blue heron walked out of the water toward me, and a squirrel played chase with a hawk. I began to realize that God still loved me, but Lily and Blanche were wearing me down. Seven days a week with no break was causing me to go crazy. I needed a way out. When I returned home I talked things over with Dean, and with the help of the nurses, hospice workers, and my sweet husband, they convinced me to place Blanche in a nursing home. This also meant that Lily could go back to Louisville.

Blanche was admitted in June 2005, and she passed away on May 18, 2006. While in the nursing home the nurses told me that she would sing hymns to them every day.

After Blanche passed away, I had a nervous breakdown and was put in a facility with a lockdown unit until I was more stable. I was watched twenty-four hours a day. The staff gave me my pills, talked to me, made me eat, and played cards with me. Since I was the only patient at the time, there was always someone with me. On my second day, they asked me to draw a butterfly. When I finished, they told me it was too pretty to hang up, so I made another one. It also was too pretty! They made me laugh, which felt good. Within three days they discharged me. I was still fragile, but I felt better. Unfortunately, my past was somehow coming back to haunt me. I was once again fearful of men. I refused to talk to a male psychiatrist, and any type of yelling gave me an unreal perception that someone was trying to hurt me.

Before long I was falling apart again, and I was readmitted to the facility. This time the institution was full of drug addicts and alcoholics—everything bad I had grown up with as a child. In spite of the fact that they reminded me of my past, I actually enjoyed my fellow wounded roommates. I even drew pictures for them. I was still frightened of men, especially the male psychiatrist. During one of my sessions, he yelled at me and asked me what I was going to do about certain situations in my life. I crumbled in my chair, shaking and frightened. Finally, he told me to leave. I ran to my room and shut the door. I then fell on my knees and told Jesus about my fears. I knew that He was the only one who could help me and rescue me from my haunting past. I prayed for a long time, asking for release and comfort. The next morning when I woke up and was greeted by my male counselor, I approached him and shook his hand. He was surprised and asked if I was afraid of him. I said, "No!" He took me to the psychiatrist, and I immediately shook his hand. We talked, and he said that I had made a complete turn around, which was unusual. I thanked my friend Jesus for once again doing the impossible.

Chapter Fifteen

One day we got a call that my dad was in the hospital. He had a hole in his intestines that had formed because he took Advil on an empty stomach. We prayed for him and tried to give him blood, but the nurse said I was HIV positive. I asked them to run the blood test again, which they did, and it came back negative. I take four medications for my asthma so that I can keep breathing, plus three other pills. My breathing medications mess up my blood tests.

While we prayed to our God to save my dad, He revealed an image of His full form to my dad on the ceiling of his hospital room. After this incident, we experienced two miracles: my dad was released from the hospital and he accepted Christ as his Savior. I was so grateful that when he passed away on December 24, 2007, in

Colorado on his way to see a daughter from his wife, Sue, that he died in Jesus. Sue, my step-mother, planned the funeral service in Colorado and did not let me know about the arrangements. Since I was unable to say goodbye to my dad, I put together a memorial for him with flowers, pictures of him riding his famous stallions, and of course the song he wrote when he was twelve years of age. We held the service at the South Louisville Seventh-day Adventist Church. Rachel and her husband, Jesse and his girlfriend, and a few other friends and family attended. Jesse gave a nice tribute and said that he admired my dad. Then I stood up and praised God for Dad's change of heart before his death.

I was still weakened and fragile, and in time I applied for disability. Of course, they denied my first request, but my attorney fought to get it approved. As part of the approval process, I had to appear in court. My counselor from the University of Louisville attended the hearing. She had seen me for years and knew me as a bubbly and happy person and now as someone who had hit rock bottom. Dean was there too.

As soon as they pushed the microphone closer to my face, I broke into tears and started babbling. The judge swore in my husband so that he could speak. The judge was very nice. They talked quite a bit, but I don't remember what was said. As the fire alarm sounded in the building, the judge stood up and said I had been disabled since 2007. I was then helped out of the courtroom.

Four months later Dean began a new job, and I was left alone in the house. I would get Dean off to work and then sit, trying to remember what fun things I liked to do. Over time God led me outside, and I began mowing seven of our fifteen acres. Among the tall weeds and grass, I found baby trees and a pink hollyhock bush. I discovered enjoyment in being outside in nature. I also found trees that were being choked to death by vines as large as a fire hose. I started cutting the vines and pulling them out of the trees. I mowed my way right up to the canyon ridge on our property where it went downhill. I found daffodils everywhere and tiger lilies all the way down into the canyon. I decided to mow a path into the canyon so that we could enjoy the beauty of the wildflowers. At the bottom of the canyon was a riverbed with all kinds of rocks and little pools of minnows. The trees, canyon, and flowers brought peace to my soul, mind, and heart. Within the woods I found wild blackberries, raspberries, and black raspberries! Rachel bought us more daffodils and two cherry bushes.

I joyfully spent time in God's creation working the land and beautifying our property. I was grateful for God's love and His promises: "Yea, I have loved thee with an everlasting love: therefore with lovingkindness have I drawn thee" (Jer. 31:3).

Chapter Sixteen

Dean and I missed Kay. We knew she had gotten married but that her precious husband had died in the hospital because of complications. She moved from California to Missouri with her husband's relatives, but that didn't work out either. She had a twin brother who stayed by her side and supported her through the crisis. One day, out of the blue, Kay called us. Dean and I got so excited. We asked where she was and what we could do for her. We sent her a package, and soon after we went to visit her.

One day she called and was concerned about news that the government was going to shut down the cities. She asked if she and her brother could come stay with us. We had dreamed of this for a long time, so we were very excited about the prospect of having Kay nearby again. We took our old '77 Ford truck and went to get her and her brother. It was truly an adventure moving them and Kay's two cats and a big dog and all their stuff. Kay drove her car, and we drove the truck. Of course, the truck broke down, but Dean fixed it in a couple of days. We also ran out of gas thirty minutes from home. I think I drove the police officer crazy trying to explain our situation. We were so tired, but we made it! Kay and her twin stayed in our three-bedroom home with our five cats until they could get settled in their own place.

Kay looked for homes, and one modular home company said if she had two acres she could build a home on it. Dean and I gave Kay and her twin 2.7 acres as a gift. God worked out all the details, and months later they moved in to their new place.

The best thing about having Kay and her brother nearby were the holidays. We didn't have much, but we didn't need much. We made gifts and just enjoyed spending extra time together. We were also blessed to often have Rachel and her husband, and Jesse and his girlfriend join us. I will always cherish those times together when we could just eat and relax and count our blessings.

We know Jesus is coming back sooner than anyone believes, so it is our deepest prayer that many will come to know our tender and loving heavenly Father. We long to leave this dying world and be with Jesus, which is where we all were meant to be before Satan kidnapped our old world. Soon after a 1,000 year Sabbath in heaven, God will bring His glorious city down to the earth and make a new world for us to enjoy.

We need not to be afraid of God. He loves us more than we know; He is determined to woo us to Himself so that we can live with Him forever. He made us, redeemed us, and loves being close to us. He wants to sing His sweet melodies to us as he holds us safe in His arms. Do you know my friend Jesus? Do you know how much He longs to hold you in His arms of love? If you don't know Him, please come to Jesus. You don't have to be afraid. His Love is stronger than anything in this old world. Come to Jesus.

We invite you to view the complete
selection of titles we publish at:

www.ASPECTBooks.com

Please write or email us your praises, reactions, or
thoughts about this or any other book we publish at:

AB ASPECT Books
www.ASPECTBooks.com

P.O. Box 954
Ringgold, GA 30736

info@ASPECTBooks.com

ASPECT Books titles may be purchased in bulk for educational,
business, fund-raising, or sales promotional use.
For information, please e-mail:

BulkSales@ASPECTBooks.com

Finally, if you are interested in seeing
your own book in print, please contact us at

publishing@ASPECTBooks.com

We would be happy to review your manuscript for free.